PRAISE FOR *DEAR GOD.*
DEAR BONES. DEAR YELLOW.

"This is a triumph of a book—one where Hindi's poems generate the kind of jolt rarely seen in a debut collection. Urgent and searing, these poems are both jocular and declamatory in all the most memorable of ways— delivering crackles of energy long after you close the book."

—Aimee Nezhukumatathil, author of *World of Wonders*

"Noor Hindi's debut is a book that knows what it is to live in many worlds at once while also occupying a singular perspective. And speaking of occu- pation—this is a book staking its right to call out those who would seek to forget the inheritance due to a displaced but dynamic people, while also celebrating all those worth loving. Armed with a journalist's heart and a poet's mind, Hindi has written blazingly toward a future where 'what's real/is us.'"

—Tarfia Faizullah, author of *Registers of Illuminated Villages*

"Noor Hindi peels the nictitating membrane between dimensions until every context is rubbing up against the next one. The eye is an open door, the world is one room and no rooms. Come in, come in. Spin out then sit down. No compartments allowed, and the clock is broken, so everything is now. We are pressing our eyeballs against the map, the mist, the moon, every mirror, every pixel, every headline. This book is funny, is tender, is moving, is sharp as hell and raises hell. Hindi names names the way a poet must, and don't you feel dared to do the same? This collection takes in history both unfolded and unfolding, yet still barrels toward the light. Where has this book been all my life? But also? Here it is. And we are so lucky."

—Jess Rizkallah, author of *the magic my body becomes*

DEAR GOD. DEAR BONES. DEAR YELLOW.

DEAR GOD. DEAR BONES. DEAR YELLOW.

Noor Hindi

Haymarket Books
Chicago, Illinois

Published in 2022 by
Haymarket Books
P.O. Box 180165
Chicago, IL 60618
773-583-7884
www.haymarketbooks.org
info@haymarketbooks.org

ISBN: 978-1-64259-696-0

Distributed to the trade in the US through Consortium Book Sales and
Distribution (www.cbsd.com) and internationally through Ingram Publisher
Services International (www.ingramcontent.com).

This book was published with the generous support of Lannan Foundation and
Wallace Action Fund.

Special discounts are available for bulk purchases by organizations and institu-
tions. Please email info@haymarketbooks.org for more information.

Cover design by Brett Neiman. Cover art: "Hello?" by Arwa Alshamsi.

Library of Congress Cataloging-in-Publication data is available.

Entered into digital printing May, 2022.

For those on the outside of the door.
Let this book be an invitation, as prayer, as love. Come in.

CONTENTS

I.

Self-Interrogation

At the airport terminal, a woman is crying.
Excuse me. Excuse me. Excuse me, I—
Need to focus. On something besides.
The rush of migration. Lights so loud.
The unending sound. Of a newscaster's voice.
Dear God. Dear Bones. Dear Mother. Please, forgive
me. I want to call in dead. Last week,
there was a child in a yellow dress reading a poem.
For minutes on end, I could not be indifferent
to anything. Not the grass, dying yellow.
Not the bombs, twisting limbs. Not the cages.
Not the—Yes. There is a woman crying
at terminal six. Yes, I use a newspaper
to cover my eyes. Yes, I think of the child.
The tiny silver heart she placed in my palm.
How I threw it in the trash, seconds later.
But I promise. I promise. I promise. I—
meant it as an act of survival. Maybe love.

Thirst

Amman was a broken
    railing I tried to lean on
        and the Athan was a song

I tried and tried to love. That summer,
    I was little and terrified
        of God, my lust hanging

from the roots of my hair.
    What did I know of the thirst
        that moved at the speed

of fingers exploring a body
    I wanted to be mine? I remember
        my grandmother

tapping her feet during iftar,
    say *al-Hamdillah*, say *I am thankful*
        for this sunlight, this sorrow,

this summer, which is endless
    and tastes like heat. After iftar,
        I would hold her hand, let her guide

me to the women's mosque,
    where dirt lined
        the soles of their feet;

their hands clutched prayer beads,
    eyes with us and not. I longed
        for the softness and surrender

that I mistook for faith.
    Oh Allah, I never found you
        in those spaces. Oh Allah,

it's true: I turned selfish. Years later
          and wanted to fuck
                    her—drank to drink

and get drunk until I was brave
          and no longer a girl
                    wiping my teeth

with pages of the Quran.
          When morning came, one of us
                    spent hours washing

her hands in an ocean of bleach,
          the other stumbled into a mosque
                    for the first time in years

and howled at Allah for creating
          appetites and tongues, for lungs
                    that inhale so much of this world.

In Which the White Woman on My Thesis Defense Asks Me about *Witness*

1. And what does it mean to *witness* yourself, on television, dying?
    a. I no longer watch the news.
    b. I've exhausted every mirror in my home searching for my eyes.
    c. I mean to talk about the intersection between a knife and the flip side of a mirror.

2. Might we define this as a collective *trauma?*
    a. Whose trauma?
    b. A gathering of bodies might be called a circus to some // and a graveyard to others.
    c. I cannot exactly describe what "this" is. // My mind sharpens // to salted lemons.

3. When you speak to your father about the politics surrounding *witness,* does he move beyond geography?
    a. I never cared for maps.
    b. My mother used to warn me: "God is watching. Your grandfather is watching. Your father is watching." Their eyeballs // a static screen // *shut off // off // off //* I scream.
    c. Whose geography?

4. Tell us about *spectacle.*
    a. You pleasure that which makes us fiction // while staring // into our graved eyes.
    b. My mother walking through Macy's.
    c. The intuitive desire to laugh at racist jokes is what my body might recognize as survival.

5. Do you believe in America?
    a. *Believe* is sister to *memory,* and to *love,* and to *cheer,* and to *trust.* There are drones outside the doors of America. Who will catch them?
    b. Who is the audience for this question?
    c. Before burial, the hearse brought my grandfather's body to our home in Akron, Ohio. Through a window, I watched the hearse take two laps around our block, then followed its license plate to disappearance.

Fuck Your Lecture on Craft, My People Are Dying

Colonizers write about flowers.
I tell you about children throwing rocks at Israeli tanks
seconds before becoming daisies.
I want to be like those poets who care about the moon.
Palestinians don't see the moon from jail cells and prisons.
It's so beautiful, the moon.
They're so beautiful, the flowers.
I pick flowers for my dead father when I'm sad.
He watches *Al Jazeera* all day.
I wish Jessica would stop texting me *Happy Ramadan.*
I know I'm American because when I walk into a room something dies.
Metaphors about death are for poets who think ghosts care about sound.
When I die, I promise to haunt you forever.
One day, I'll write about the flowers like we own them.

I Once Looked in a Mirror but Couldn't See My Body

after Ghassan Kanafani

I document as argument; I exist.
I learn this from watching my father

alone in the night
drawing and redrawing
a map
of Palestine, green ink.

Before 1947, he would insist, *before partition,*
before the nation became history,

before my tongue mistook *thank you* for survival,

before I chose an industry that headlines
my people dead.

A camera melts in the desert sun.
From far away, I hear the dying clicks of its shutter, the loud bang of
    headlines slamming
newspapers, the sharp gaze of eyeballs.

Standing before my father, my own pupils gaping
at his calloused hands, I too wish to capture this moment,

hold it. Say, *yes, this violence is possible*, and also, *there is pleasure*
in looking.

But who is the audience of my looking
and how far does a hurt stretch
before it yellows?

Breaking [News]

We'll wake up, Sunday morning, and read the paper. Read each other.

Become consumers

of each other's stories—a desperate reaching

for another body's warmth, its words buoying us through a world. We carry
   graveyards on our

backs, and I'm holding a lightning bug

hostage in one hand, its light dimming in the warmth

of my fist, and in the other, a pen, to document its death. *Isn't that terrible?*
   I'll ask you, shutting

my fist once more.

In interviews, I frame my subject's stories through a lens to make them
   digestible to consumers.

I become a machine. A transfer of information. The stories—a plea for
   empathy—an over

saturation of feelings we'll fail at transforming into action.

What's lost is incalculable.

   And at the end of summer, the swimming pools will be gutted of water.

   And it'll be impossible to swim.

Palestine

is a woman. A child
in a thobe. Olive pits in
my hands. The tatreez
on my grandmother's scarf.
Is thirty-four Palestinians killed.
We don't wake up. American
politicians. Occupied
country. *Israel has the right
to defend itself.* Ahed Tamimi,
ice cream on tongue,
flavor unknown. *Are you grateful
your parents came to
this country?* Three hundred
dead. Open-air prison. Ten-year
blockade. Rouzan al-Najjar,
accidental bullet. Pomegranate
so bloody. My grandmother,
born ten days before Nakba,
gunpowder in her blood.
Stop killing us.
Stop telling us how to fight.
Is grape mint hookah, country
I've never visited. Woman,
body bruised and policed.
Is queer. Is *fuck the patriarchy.*
Is three hundred thousand Palestinians killed.
My father crying
to Omayma El Khalil. Sweet black tea,
fresh mint stuck on the roof
of my mouth. Two state "solution."
*We thought the house
was empty.* Is stranger living
in my great-grandfather's home,
eating the pomegranates he once planted.
So how do you say

your name again? Is
????? Palestinians killed. Sunflowers
on their graves. Seeds
we crack between our teeth,
spitting out each shell
before digging another grave.

Broken Light Bulb Flickering Away

Every week I fall in love
with a new bad idea. I hope
one day to magic my body
away. I wish for everyone to leave
me alone and talk to me
at once. Please,
forgive me. All I've ever wanted
is to be the poet laureate
of Flamin' Hot Cheetos. All my desires
go unnoticed. On my birthday, I visit a fortune-teller.
She tells me *beware of the letter J.*
Jackhammers. Joylessness. Jukeboxes.
White men named Jason. Jesus,
there is so much junk in my brain.
My father escaped war,
and here I am, the perfect
immigrant child. I assimilate so much
I drink Diet Coke
at the rate of a middle-aged
white woman. My mother wanted
to be a writer. I should hold
her sacrifices but instead sob
into a donut decorated like the US flag
at 3 a.m. My cat is tired of my antics.
My parents named me *Light* because
their lives lie in shadow
but I'm a poor example of joy.
Sometimes I get so sad
I think about eating a quesadilla,
or assembling a tire swing,
or taking off my bra. Instead I dream
of the big dumb heart my mother
hands me. She tells me to carry it.
I drop it every time.

Self-Portrait as Arab/Muslim Teenager
in an All-White High School

I ride my camel to class every day.

I have oil on oil on oil

hidden in my backpack

   along with bombs!!!!!!!

(I'm joking! I'M JOKING . . . . i'm joking lol)

   EVERYBODY SING ALONG

We Gettin' Arab Money—

feelsafefeelsafefeelsafefeelsafe.

Ask me if I'm Arabic.

Ask me if my dad is Osama bin Laden.

   Ask me to pledge allegiance

      to a moon that won't answer my calls.

      Dear Ms. Wright plz don't ban
      my flying carpet—

Jesus Christ. Jesus Christ. Jesus.

      I die
while reading *The Catcher in the Rye.*

         ThE cArousEL WOulD nOT stop SpinNiNG—
   So I murder Holden Caulfield
         -Because your canon ain't shit //
         compared to Ghassan Kanafani-

   Someday, I'll run for President!!!!!!

I tell the vice principal

before getting expelled.

Good Muslims Are All Around Us

after Jillian Weise

Blindfolded Muslim Man Gives Free Hugs in Wake of Manchester City Center

"Muslim Spiderman" to Get French Citizenship after Saving Child

Muslims Love Jesus Too

US Woman Who "Hated Muslims" Now Wants to Share the Love and Understanding She Found in an Afghan Refugee

Young Muslims Wake Up Early to Clean Up the Streets after New Year's Celebration

Muslims Raise $250,000 for Pittsburgh Synagogue

Muslims and Jews Come Together So They Can Serve One Thousand Bowls of Soup to the Homeless

Muslim Father Forgives Man Involved with Son's Murder, Hugs Him in Court

Muslim Teen Assists Police in Arrest of Man Who Assaulted Jewish Woman

Muslim-Owned Restaurant Offers Free Christmas Meal for Homeless and Elderly

Muslims Come to Times Square to Take Stand against Extremism

British Train passengers Jump to Defend Muslim Sisters from Hate

Muslim Woman Disarms Anti-Islam Protester with a Hug

Far-Right Protestors Make Friends with Muslims After Being Invited for Tea

Report Says War Waning in Muslim World Speaking Up: Young Muslims Confront Extremism

American Muslims Determined to Counter Violent Extremism

Most Muslims "Desire Democracy"

Chicago's Non-Muslim Schoolgirls Wear Hijabs to Promote Acceptance of Islamic Beliefs

Mosque Helps Vandalized Church Clean Up

Man Who Threatened to Kill Ilhan Omar Given Lighter Sentence After She Asks for Compassion

Some Good News About Muslims in Europe

Muslim Group Hands Out One Thousand Holiday Turkey Meals to Needy Families

Man Who Shot Up Mosque Goes Back for Forgiveness, Finds Hugs Waiting

Muslim Restaurant Owner Finds and Turns in Bag with $100,000 Cash

Priest Allows Muslims to Chant Islamic Supremacy Prayer During Mass

Muslims Should Disarm Islamophobia with Kindness

Breaking [News]

Reporting is an act of violence—poetry one of warmth.
I own so many cameras.
      Televisions. Notebooks. Pens.

There's a woman standing inside of a bus,
where an act of violence occurs.
      I record. I interview. I document. I see

violence between the bright blue lines of my margins.
      I tell myself it's enough.

Dear victim of capitalism, of oppression, of police brutality,
      of racism, of misogyny, of America, of colonialism—

/////You are more than the shadow I write you through/////
      /////There are sunflowers sprouting from your hands/////

In five minutes or less, please look
into this camera and answer to the following—

      [starts sobbing]

When I wake up, I am the flashing red stage lights
shooting over my subject.

      [continues sobbing]

A Day, A Life: When a Medic Was Killed in Gaza, Was It an Accident?

for Rouzan al-Najjar
after / in defiance of a piece published by the New York Times *about al-Najjar*

And what about the flowers
   on her scarf? Her white
      medical coat, now red?

Nails painted pink
   as a tongue, a sunset,
      a pomegranate? How tear gas

forms clouds above
   the dead. How a land—
      force-fed bullets and blood—

ruptures its stomach
   and swings it at a flag.
      Tell me why my people's

deaths become a *hopeless, endless*
   conflict and the lives war wastes.
      What murders become *accident,*

unintentional in the eyes
   of those who name my father's tears
      an unending and insolvable

cycle of violence. Tell me about the thirty witness
   interviews and one thousand photos and videos
      it took for you to name our resistance

as *drama.* Tell me. In a country that allows four hours
   of electricity a day, how a people live
      in darkness, hold the keys to homes

blown up by soldiers, while a mother
   clutches her daughter, now dead, takes off
      Rouzan's white gloves, grieves the sun

and its impenetrable light. Remembers
   the toy stethoscopes Rouzan played
      with as a child, then stares

into the eyes of an Israeli soldier.
   And laughs.

Grief Symphony

for Israa Ghrayeb

Dear olive tree // how much red
have you seen? // Can you hold Israa's
too? // Remember those men
with fists // in the air // then fists
pounding skin // bruises
not yellowed? // I hung
cherries on your branches // pits
in my teeth // If you slice a cherry open,
there's a heart, beating // & sweet.

Breaking [News]

We know death
is futile know death
as 3.5 thousand
retweets a trauma
a thing named
empty in internet
measured in the slow
bend of your fingers
clicking the quiet
tempo of expiration
your spleen
in the shape of a gun
in the shape of a pen
I am going
door to door
collecting stories
I place a tape recorder
at the edge of a child's
stroller and watch
her position it between her teeth
chew on story
and argue she's agent
of her own story
I dream of America
as nightmare
as child placing drone
in mouth as mother
placing drone
in child's mouth
to condition her tongue
to the taste
of America I see you
door to door
in eviction
court I attend

and a judge asks
to see
my face so I show her
my blood at the edge
of survival
an audience
of w(h)it(e)ness
Sir, why
are you being evicted
which system
what history
I know your trauma
is a thing we'll name
breaking
news your trauma
a hunger we crave
your trauma behind a paywall
your trauma we measure
with clicks I document
futility to feed America
more story muddled
by story there is a child
crying in front of a pink wall
as her home is demolished
in Palestine
it moves one to tears
to watch
your own reflection
on a screen
your face in anguish
at another's pain
looks so sweet
almost heroic.

I Buried My Brother Last Winter

After the last overdose, I prayed my brother
would die. My hands became knives. I watched

my father pace back and forth, watched
my siblings become a terror

of secrets submerged in snow. My mother, the broken piano.
I, the pianist, smashed my fingers

against her keys, an audience waiting in suspense
for a moment of reprieve. I've parted

with compassion. The first time I met my father,
I was interviewing a Bhutanese refugee.

I don't know where my sons are. We don't speak
the same language. They come home

late. I want to apologize on behalf of all children
of refugees. We leave our shoes on the doors of America

and come back to find them bleeding. Where is my brother now?
On a 911 call, *what is the location of your emergency?*

I want to say home, but my body is a lost signal.
Is there a gun at the residence?

No ma'am, except for the one I'm pointing at him
in a photo years ago,

where my father's hand is rested on his shoulders,
holding him still, for the last time in forever.

Breaking [News]

I'm not a poet anymore—
I've interviewed too many politicians.
All they care for is ghosts.
Breaking news, I'm breaking
up with my stupid shame.
I have dates on my calendar
just for fucking. I do this
between my 9-5. *Hello, hello.*
I'm quieter than I seem.
I'm a man in a suit.
Please pass the damn hookah.
Please tell the politicians I'm tired
of reporting. We're all terrible. My desire
to fix this window is corrupt. Your desire
to call your looking through this window
an act of social justice is corrupt.
At a protest, a white woman calls me fake news.
Okay, fine, I tell her back. I don't smile
anymore. I do the job so well
I out cry the eagles. I out run
the sad. I trouble
my brain into a blender
then hand you a cup.
My mother holds a butterfly
to the sky.
White-winged, glimmering mess.
Someone, please, snap a photo.
My shoes are drenched in blood.

All My Plants Are Dead

I stopped trying

to feed anything but myself.

I woke up yesterday and couldn't see

a road, then I woke up the next day

and someone gave me a book

about male entitlement

which I drowned in orange juice.

I am trying to be more even tempered.

I am trying to eat my Craisins in peace.

I think I would like

to have the memory of a dog.

It would make me more forgiving.

Someone tells me to imagine

my troubles as leaves floating

away in a river so I ask them why

men have giant mouths,

and there I go again fucking

things up with my politics.

Yesterday a white guy tried

telling me what it's like to be a woman

of color, so I placed my hands

in his mouth and ruptured his vocal cords.

I am not a political person.

Let's talk about the moon.

It's so pretty tonight.

No. Fuck that. I am the moon.

II.

AMERICAN BEINGS

Confession

We did not watch baseball. My siblings learned English by watching *Full House*. As a child, I learned how to dip pita bread into hummus, zait & za'atar, labneh, baba ghanoush. My family comes from a land that does not exist on colonizers' maps. In my earliest memories, my father is running the blade of a knife down a prickly pear. A pomegranate. I knew football as fútbol, not soccer. Microsoft Word would like to correct this. Sometimes I remember standing on the rooftop patio in Amman, the city engulfed in light, hanging from the clouds. My uncle was undocumented. We lived in Section 8 housing. We are Muslim & sometimes we joked about blowing shit up. Sometimes my father couldn't afford school supplies. We ate ketchup sandwiches. My grandmother's name is *Jihad*. I don't like the Middle East. I don't like America. I drank too many Little Hug Fruit Barrels as a kid, high fructose corn syrup painted my lips.

A Prayer

My mother is a blue apron pacing in the kitchen. My mother is speaking in prayer for my undocumented uncle. She hangs our clothes on a clothesline. She washes a plate.

I hear her whisper, بدون أوراق, *without papers*, to my father when talking about my uncle.

The first time I meet him, he's just arrived from Amman, Jordan, to our home in Barberton, Ohio. He's loud. He talks fast. His arms flail in the air when he makes a joke. His legs bounce and he has a nervous habit of brushing his nose with his index finger when telling a story. He is unlike my mother, who moves quietly through our home.

I'm about four years old when I meet him. Each Friday, after finishing his shift at a gas station, he fills a plastic bag with candy and brings it home to us. He makes my mother laugh. He reminds her of home.

He will be بدون أوراق for a long, long time. It will feel like forever.

A Question

A child asks:

"If aliens invaded Earth, wouldn't we seem alien to them?"

According to the US Citizenship and Immigration Services (USCIS), in the US, you are an *alien* if you are not a US citizen. If you hold a green card (permanent resident card), you are considered a *resident alien*.

alien (adjective)

1. a: belonging or relating to another person, place, or thing:

   STRANGE *//an alien* environment

   b: relating, belonging, or owing allegiance to another country or government: FOREIGN *//alien* residents

   c: EXOTIC *//alien* plants

   d: coming from another world: EXTRATERRESTRIAL

// *alien* being

// an *alien* spaceship

alien (noun)

1. a: a person of another family, race, or nation

   //aliens seeking asylum in the US

   b: a foreign-born resident who has not been naturalized and is still a subject or citizen of a foreign country

//Alien//Alone//(UN)natural//

My grandmother is ALIEN. My father is ALIEN. My mother is ALIEN. I am ALIEN. My siblings are ALIEN. The whole goddamn world is ALIEN.

My God. We are all

So green. Have you looked

at the grass?

USCIS Trip #1: A Revision

At the USCIS office in Cleveland, Ohio, my grandmother and I move through security. We are here to get her fingerprints scanned so she can become a US citizen. My grandmother has held a green card for five years. She's lived with my parents during her time here, and travels back and forth from Jordan to the US.

Over the last year, we've finished her USCIS Form N-400 and sent it in, along with the $725 fee.

We ride the elevator to the fifth floor. The federal building is cold and stale. My grandmother is draped in her black abaya. She clutches her purse. Light brown eyes wait for the doors to open.

A white woman greets us at the door, then slides a form under the green glass screen for us to fill out. Our reflections stare back.

When asked about her country of origin, my grandmother writes PALESTINE in black pen and slides it back to the woman.

The white woman says WE DO NOT RECOGNIZE

PALESTINE AS A COUNTRY

TRY AGAIN

And crosses out PALESTINE with a red pen.

A Quick Study of the Word *Existence*

My father pronounces the letter *p* as *b* because the sound *p* doesn't exist in the Arabic alphabet.

To exist comes from the Latin existere/exsister, "to step out, stand forth, emerge, appear."

I argue: I exist. Palestine exists. Undocumented immigrants exist. Muslims exist.

My desire to make this argument is rooted in America's desire to erase me.

Who is the audience for my argument, exactly?

Yesterday, my father saved three plump figs in the fridge for me.

Today, I will eat them while standing in our kitchen, my shadow dancing on the walls, my body warm—like sunlight.

Tapping on the Glass

There were about fifty mailboxes in Section 8 housing in Barberton. The mailboxes were in the middle of the large roundabout in front of our home. Behind the mailboxes was an enclosed bulletin board for announcements and flyers.

No one ever used the bulletin board. Or, I never paid attention. It's the bees I fixated on. They were trapped behind the sliding glass doors. So many of them. Dead. Bee corpses everywhere. A few flew around, hitting the glass doors again and again.

I watched them all the time. I didn't care about helping them escape. When I'd get bored, which was often, I liked tapping on the glass and shaking the foundation of the board and watching the bees fly in circles and panic. I don't know how they got in, but I knew they couldn't leave. If I pressed my ear to the glass, I could hear them buzzing, drones.

USCIS Trip #2: Violation

I stand in front of my grandmother. We are here so she can be interviewed by an immigration officer. First, police scanners and metal detectors.

TAKE OFF YOUR SHOES
MAKE SURE YOU HAVE YOUR ID ON HAND
NO BELTS, PHONES, JACKETS

I wonder why the officers are always yelling. One of the officers wants to check my hair, has flagged me for "additional screening." I have to stand with my hands up as he waves a scanner around my body.

When I turn around, my grandmother is not wearing her headscarf. I'm not used to seeing her golden-brown hair in public. I give her a questioning look as she waits for her black headscarf to move through the security monitor.

When I ask her what happened, she won't look at me. Keeps whispering, "شلحونئ, شلحونئ"—*they stripped me, they stripped me.* She hurries her scarf around her head. Tells me an officer demanded she take it off, twice.

I want my rage to elicit love and more love. I want people to stop asking if I love this country. No. Ask if it loves me.

On the way home that day, it is autumn and the leaves are beautiful and dying. My grandmother watches the trees through the passenger window.

I want her to want more from America.
شلحونئ
شلحونئ
شلحونئ

The words pound in my head. My anger, a sound I turn down like a bad song no one wants to listen to.

She asks me to look at the trees. I tell her I am looking.

The Dream

My mom, standing at the door of our house in Barberton, wearing a bleach-stained t-shirt, her curly hair swaying in the sunlight, calling my name to come home.

Dad calling me an old lady for drinking the leftover sweet black tea each morning. His laughter, an echo. His head cradled back. Eyes full.

Making mud soup with my friend, Shawnee, her scrawny body leaning over a plastic bowl, her hand holding a stick as she swirls it through the mud.

Lying next to my dad as I fall asleep, the sound of *Al Jazeera* booming through the living room, my hair smelling like cool watermelon L'Oréal Kids shampoo.

I'm about thirteen years old when we move to our house in Akron. I tell my brother I miss our home in Barberton. He says, "We lived in the fucking projects." When we buy our house in Akron, it's not the home of my parents' American Dream. It's foreclosed. It's Akron. It's not the richer neighboring counties of my mother's wishes.

The house is a wreck. The bathrooms need updating. A kitchen needs built. The windows need replaced. The hardwood floors need refinished. The grass cut. The walls repainted.

A white picket fence needs building. It's missing a two-car garage. A white family. An SUV. Two kids, blonde hair and blue eyes.

To this day, she calls our home a خرابة, *a desolation.*

USCIS Trip #3: A Test

My grandma has to memorize the questions and answers for the USCIS civics test. She doesn't speak much English, but she reads well. For months, she carries her study booklet everywhere she goes, and alternates between memorizing the questions and reading the Quran.

At USCIS, the officer will ask her ten random questions out of a selection of one hundred. She has to answer at least six correctly.

What is the "rule of law"?
What happened at the Constitutional Convention?

I test her every week for two months, and every day when we get closer to the date. She has trouble pronouncing four words: *legislature, communism, terrorist,* and *spangled*. The night before her test, I repeat them to her:

legislaturecommunismterroristspangled

and she repeats them back

legislaturecommunismterroristspangled

and while sitting in the waiting room of USCIS

legislaturecommunismterroristspangled

and on and on and on

A Chaos of Semantics

Semantic satiation: A psychological phenomenon in which repetition causes a word or phrase to lose meaning, temporarily. Or, according to Urban Dictionary, it's when "you say a word so much it starts to sound fucking weird."

Leon James, a professor of psychology at the University of Hawaii, coined the term and describes the process as a kind of mental "fatigue."

I repeat:

We Too Are American We Too Are American We Too Are American We Too Are American We Too Are American We Too Are American We Too Are American We Too Are American

The words *we* and *too* push out of my mouth, like whistles. My lips stick together to produce the *ummm* in American, before the quick movements of my tongue make *erican*.

Umm. Air. Ee. Can.

When I repeat this phrase, my body disappears.

If I keep repeating it, will it render my family into existence? To whom?

I want to believe language matters, that words create meaning, that a person can breathe a thing into existence.

But what happens when the repetition of the words beckons at the opposite?

We are not

American.

I've gone on for too long.

What I'm talking about is loneliness.

A Home

The breakfast table is my family's connection to Palestine, to home, to Jordan. Eating is sacred—dipping pita bread into olive oil, an act of love.

Saturday mornings, you'll find pita bread atop the stove, my mother's hands flipping each loaf above the flames, her warmth filling us.

The homeland is stuck in our teeth. It's filling our cavities. It rests on our

tongues. My God. How we yearn for its olive trees. How it haunts our dreams.

How it—

USCIS Trip #4: A Photo

My grandmother's body in perfect posture, sitting across from an immigration officer at USCIS. A plaque on the wall in his office, a certificate of "achievement" for his time serving as a border control agent.

Six years.

The same amount of time it's taken my grandmother to get to this point.

He asks her six questions. I have the answers memorized. Their exact phrasing. The placement of their commas, their punctuation.

I sit in perfect posture. Suspended. Waiting.

When he tells my grandmother she's passed her civics test, she cries.

I try to sidestep the heaviness in the room, the violence of this moment, the violence that renders my grandmother's tears and her desire to become American.

Outside, my grandmother wants to take a photo next to the large statue of George Washington. She has her hands up, swaying in the wind. A smile sprawled on her face, laughing.

She tells me, *this is George Washington.*

I know, Grandma, I say. *I know.*

I take the photo.

III.

Poem in Which My Mother Tells Me Not to Get a Pap Smear Because It Might Tear My Nonexistent Hymen

And I'm like . . . *what about cancer . . .?*
And she's like . . . *but your hymen?*
And I say . . . *but what about death??*
And she says . . . *but the patriarchy . . .?!*
And I'm like . . . *yeah yeah, the patriarchy!*
And she's like . . . *yes, yes. Death.*

Virginity for Sale

And there was something about T. I.'s hymen???

no no no—

    (BOGUS VIRGINITY TESTS)

      What we were talking about is T. I.'s *daughter's* hymen

        whether it was intact, like, you know . . .

But then these HUMMINGBIRDS came out of nowhere

      (THE FUCK WAS HE TALKING ABOUT?)

            like WHOOOOOSHHHH

        [was my father shooting
          at the hummingbirds?]

    (T. I.'S NOT THE ONLY ONE)

     And a phone rang
      and a guy wanted to know
        if the doctors could perform
          a virginity check

             (UNFOLLOWS DAD
             ON TWITTER)

    There was SCREAMING in the background

[was that my sister?]

    Was someone about to die???
          Well actually he was joking
   had just addressed hymen-gate at a Red

(VIRGINITY CAPSULES THAT OOZE OUT
FAKE BLOOD)

Table Talk

[my sister liked hummingbirds]

And then a girl showed up

I swear he didn't touch me
I swear he didn't touch me
I swear he didn't touch me

(HYMEN HEIST)

wanted to know if we could lie to her parents????????????

but I couldn't hear her over

(GIRLS, YOU CAN NOW BUY "VIRGINITY PILLS" TO FAKE IT ON
WEDDING NIGHT) the hummingbirds

beaks so red

bodies blue

(SORRY HATERS)

(VIRGIN PASSENGERS ARE QUARANTINED
AT GATWICK AIRPORT)

fluttering about

like there was something

they couldn't escape.

In a Dream, I Get Married in an Abandoned Mall

We don't order cake. I see a dragon
graffitied on a wall. In the distance,

Archie the Snowman melts
and a guy named Fred places CAUTION

signs everywhere. We don't speak
about the bullet holes,

or the broken carousel spinning
around and around. My fiancé

is the type of Arab man
who thinks smoking double apple hookah

is a personality trait, probably
can't find the clitoris, and went to school

to become a surgeon but later settled
on dentistry. At one point, I look at him

and whisper, *I don't remember agreeing
to this shit?* He tells me not to worry,

reminds me he's a doctor, knows a lot
about cavities. There are birthday

balloons scattered everywhere and I spot
a blimp through a small window.

My wedding dress is short, so my mother
reminds me to close my legs. But I remember

I'm on my period, so I'm jamming
a $5 bill into vending machines

to purchase tampons and Snickers.
When the machines die, I punch my fiancé

in the face, and we're both shocked
at how cathartic it all feels. Shortly after,

I hijack the blimp. My teeth become a white picket fence.
I wake up as a tattered coat hanging

in the closet of my parents' first home.

Dangerous Business

My mother found a tampon wrapper THE DANGEROUS BUSINESS OF HYMEN RECONSTRUCTION SURGERIES as a child, she wouldn't let me use tampons because she was afraid of HYMEN OBSESSIONS: A HISTORICAL OVERVIEW my hymen being penetrated I FEEL BAD FOR THESE WOMEN THEY'RE FEELING SO MUCH PRESSURE FROM THEIR MALE FAMILY MEMBERS we did not talk about sex it was a thing you just didn't do AND THEY'RE AFRAID OF BEING REJECTED—OR EVEN WORSE the first time I used a tampon it was because I was on my period and I was afraid BECOME VICTIMS OF SERIOUS PHYSICAL VIOLENCE to bleed through my bathing suit which I wasn't even permitted to wear OR EVEN MURDER I had to sneak out of the house with my bathing suit in my purse I had to change at a friend's house AND DO NOT APPROACH UNLAWFUL SEXUAL INTERCOUSE. INDEED at the pool I did not know how to swim, but I jumped in anyway and clung to two pool noodles: one red and one purple HAVE A QUESTION ABOUT HYMENOPLASTY? WANT MORE INFORMATION? when I put the tampon in for the first time I did it wrong ARE CREDIT CARDS ACCEPTED FOR HYMEN REPAIR SURGERY? and I put it in wrong the second time too ARE FINANCING PLANS AVAILABLE? it was all very awkward I kept thinking I'm too old for this shit and trying to jam it in I wasn't sure what to do with all the wrappers so I started eating them MUSLIM WOMEN BUYING FAKE HYMENS TO PRETEND TO THEIR NEW HUSBANDS THEY'RE VIRGINS when I finally got one in it made me very nervous I wanted to pull it out I started tugging at the little string tug tug tug but it wouldn't come out THE WOMAN NEEDS TO SHOW PAIN. THAT IS EXACTLY WHAT THE MAN EXPECTS I thought it would be in my vagina forever swimming in its shame AS PER THE BBC AN HONOR KILLING IS THE MURDER OF A PERSON ACCUSED OF BRINGING SHAME UPON HIS OR HER FAMILY finally I yanked it out and there it swayed in the air a bloody and lifeless thing which I stared at for a while before twirling it round and round with my index finger JORDAN HAS ONE OF THE HIGHEST RATES OF HONOR CRIMES IN THE WORLD singing *there there little tampon you're just an embodiment of my shame* ACCORDING TO HUMAN RIGHTS WATCH, AROUND FIFTEEN TO TWENTY WOMEN ARE KILLED EACH YEAR when I got my period for the first time I was not taught anything about my body I was told not to touch the Quran so I learned very quickly periods are dirty women are dirty our bodies are dirty MANY JORDAN TEENAGERS SUPPORT HONOR KILLINGS after I finished staring at my tampon I cleaned it with dove soap I scrubbed extra hard but it would not get clean you could still see a little pink on the edges THE UNITED NATIONS ESTIMATES THAT AROUND FIVE THOUSAND WOMEN ARE KILLED ANNUALLY IN HONOR-RELATED CRIMES IN JORDAN, WOMEN CONSIDERED TO BE AT RISK CAN BE DETAINED INDEFINITELY UNDER THE COUNTRY'S 1954 CRIME PREVENTION LAW so I applied toothpaste and brushed it like a tooth SOME SPEND YEARS IN PRISON but it would not get clean would not get clean would not get clean ARTICLE 208 OF THE JORDANIAN PENAL CODE MEANS THAT A RAPIST CAN ESCAPE PUNISHMENT IF HE AGREES TO MARRY HIS VICTIM eventually I gave up on the tampon and flushed it down the toilet watched it swirl for a while LAWS THAT ALLOW RAPISTS TO MARRY THEIR VICTIMS COME FROM COLONIALISM, NOT ISLAM when my mother found a tampon wrapper she asked if I was a virgin I said yes yes yes yes yes yes yes yes yes yes yes yes yes yes yes yes yes yes yes yes yes yes yes yes yes yes yes yes yes yes yes

I Should Have Broken Up with My Ex

at a restaurant named Redfin Blues. Pittsburgh feels like a great place to end a relationship. It was 90 degrees. The restaurant sat on a waterfront but the water was brown. The sun wouldn't come down. I wore shorts. My boyfriend called himself a feminist. He was addicted to Pokémon GO. I wanted to hold his hand at dinner. It was way too hot to be outside. He was half-Egyptian and half-Palestinian. He called himself a feminist. We sat at a red metal table and ate shrimp. I ordered a Moscow Mule. I picked up the check. He called himself a feminist. Earlier that day, I watched him pray in an air-conditioned room. I pretended I was on my period and described my blood leaking out of my vagina. I did not want to pray. His name was Mohammad, and he prayed five times a day and he called himself a feminist. At a restaurant named Redfin Blues, I could tell he was uncomfortable with my not-praying. I could tell he was uncomfortable with my Moscow Mule. He called himself a feminist. The water around us was brown. I followed him around for days. Watched him catch Pokémon. Pretended I was interested. His name was Mohammad and he was like all the other Mohammads. My mother liked him. We were in Pittsburgh. It was 90 degrees. My father approved of him. He called himself a feminist. On the way out of the restaurant, he made a comment about my shorts. He said they were too short. He said they made him jealous. He called himself a feminist. I wanted to break up with him. He called himself a feminist. It was 90 degrees. I should have thrown him in the water. I should have smeared my fake period blood all over his face. The water was so dirty. I couldn't stop looking. All the fish died. It was 90 degrees. I didn't want to swim.

Summertime

I've carried a "Keep Calm, Carry On" bookmark in my pocket for the last
   twenty-two days.
Everyone wants to shake my hand.
Hello, my name is Light.
Look at how quickly I can love, unlove, pretend to love.
The sound of conversation.
I once killed
A lot of bees with a plastic bat.
They invaded my friend's backyard.
Tiny sunlights quivering in the air,
they were relentless, and it seemed we could fight for an unending number
   of days.
I was nine and the bees were dying and we called my massacre bravery.
Have you ever gazed at the center of a sunflower?
It's so beautiful it should eat us.
Alive.
Yesterday, I dreamed I was fixing an elevator.
It only went up—
forever and ever, but I grew tired of its constant optimism.
The persistence of everything,
sometimes it kills me.

I Call My Mother from the Moon

I say Guess What?
I Made It
To the Moon. And
It's Stunning. And
I Miss You. And
You'd Love the View
From Up Here.
Men Don't Exist.
I can tell by the way
she pauses
she's worried. She asks
But How Will You
Bear Children
In A Place with No
Gravity? How
Am I To Find You
A Good Man
From Up There?
Get Down Here.
I Need to Teach You
How to Make
A Good Cake.
Your Future Son
Will Be Beautiful
Like You.
Please, Come Down.
I Miss You.
I Taught You
To Be Quieter
Than This, Less
Hungry
For the World
So You Could Fit
Inside a World
Unfit for Women

Like Us.
There is air.
Until there isn't.
I've always wanted more
than the world
she gave me.
Up here, my eyes grow
larger. I bake a cake.
It floats away.
I wish she were here.
To catch it.

The Shell of a Cactus Fruit

Dear K,

Have you dreamed of pomegranates this week. You always talk of the pome-
granate trees that reflected from your grandfather's eyes. If history is a woman
with gentle hands pouring black tea, let there be sunlight, a soft chair, a
young Palestinian boy entering his home for the first time. Let the woman
be Jewish, and let there be nothing political about the way she yearns for her
son's safety, about the years between 1948 and 1974, years your grandfather
spent mourning the dirt in which he planted those pomegranate trees. In this
version of history, there is some forgiveness. *Come in, come in,* she beckons
you. You enter. Everything will change.

Dear K,

All this is real. You tell me stories. You repeat *did you get that?* and *do you hear me?* like I won't believe you. You hate the way I interrupt *Al Jazeera*, how I seek answers to questions I shouldn't be asking. Your body is collapsed on our tired beige couch. Every hour we talk makes me wonder if you'll ever make eye contact. *Will you look at me?* Palestinian habits die because Palestinians are dying—are dead. It happens every day. I know you think of your grandfather, how he spent so many of his days staring at a ceiling, inhaling cigarette smoke, relying on the United Nations for food, for shelter. Year after year, you hovered around him—unbreakable.

Dear K,

You told me once he would smack fear right out of you. In a memory, an Israeli soldier lines you against a wall. Threatens to shoot. Your friend pees himself while waiting for death's sweet respite, warm urine flows down his legs.

In another memory, the six-day war rages. What you remember is the smell of fire, the sweet mulberries staining your teeth after days of migration.

Years later, I will ask you for these memories again. You will ask me where I've gotten them. *Maybe I've dreamed them*, I'll tell you. Later, you'll wash your hands. I'll notice purple juice coursing through the crevices on your palms, the smell of mulberries in the kitchen. An unfamiliar face.

Dear K,

I remember the cactus fruits you would always bring home. The shell of the cactus fruit has hundreds of hair-like thorns hiding under its surface. You always knew the exact place the blade of the knife must slice to open the sweet part of the fruit. Is that not love?

Ode

Edgewater Beach, 2019
  for Kevin

The night, so warm I could fall in love
with anything
including myself. My loves, you are the only people
I'd surrender my softness to.
The moon so blue. What's gold
is gold. What's real
is us despite
a country so grieved, so woke, so deathly.
Our gloom as loud as shells.
Listen. Even the ocean begs.
Put your hands in the sand, my friend.
It's best we bury ourselves.
What's heavy. What's heavy?
Becomes light.

Dabke

A child loses a frisbee in the water. In her grief,
she continues to play, pretends to toss
an invisible thing into the ache, all castle.
It's impossible to feel depressed at the beach.
The waves too persistent. The sky a zig-zag
of look. The sand cannot be displaced.
In a new city, I find my people. I love.
Yet we do not solve a single thing. Not
the occupation, a freeze. Not the guns,
flying howl, not the—not the—not.
Someone says all resistance is futile. And yet
we plunge into the yellow weep—
And linger.

IV.

Pledging Allegiance

I am tired of language. I don't want to make metaphors. About olive trees. About wearing a keffiyeh. About About About. The dream has not ended. My grandma is back in Jordan. She loves her passport. What does it mean to love? A country? A book? A people? To say "I absolutely and entirely renounce and abjure all allegiance and fidelity to any foreign prince, potentate, state, or sovereignty," while thinking about Palestine. While holding the key to your father's first home. While While While. The news keeps screaming. The headlines chew at our eyes. A bald eagle burdens its wings with suitcases, then drops them in another land.

The language isn't enough.

Here—an image of homeland. The word *colonization*, a photo of a fruit so bloodied. I hold a beam of light to a wall, make shadows of Palestine I try to catch. Olive tree, Israeli soldier, a metaphor of Palestine as a woman.

In workshop, a white classmate says *some of us celebrate diversity.* Someone wants to talk about hummus and falafel (pronounces them both wrong, then asks me for the labor of forgiveness).

I'm supposed to be feeding them whatever is the opposite of guilt. I want to move beyond. Where?

There are bodies. And then there are fewer bodies. This is the formula.

Ask me about a two-state solution. About caring for a world that does not love you back. About holding a knife and tearing into a map. But oh—

There's the cliché again. But the deaths. But the deaths. But the deaths. Have they, too, become a cliché? A transgender Palestinian teen is stabbed. Israa Ghrayeb is dead. Gazan families continue to face an electricity crisis.

And still—*I didn't even know any of this was happening. // Thank you for educating me. // Do you like living in America? // But what about those terrorists? // When you say Palestine, do you actually mean Pakistan?*

What comes after awareness? And then what? And then what? There's a bird. No, it's a drone. My tax dollars pay for the bombs that kill my people.

I'm locked out of my home. No, I can't recognize my home. I grabbed the wrong keys. The house has been painted a different color. There is music inside but I don't understand the words. There is smoke inside, but nothing is burning.

All I do is wait. I peer in from the windows. The house is inhabited by ghosts. They recognize my face but not my tongue. I try to find where it hurts.

The ghosts laugh. Their laughs end with a sharp pang of grief; it sounds like a fist, or a hand around my throat. I reach for them, begging to be let in. When I ring the bell, no one answers. I draw letters on the outside of the door.

ACKNOWLEDGMENTS

Thank you, Mary Biddinger, Caryl Pagel, Hilary Plum, and David Giffels, for your support, wisdom, and guidance. Thank you, George Abraham, Randa Jarrar, Fargo Tbakhi, Summer Farah, and Ruth Awad, as well as the folks at Radius of Arab American Writers for finding me. Thank you, Kevin Latimer, D. T. McCrea, Geramee Hensley, and J. David, as well as the Sad Kid Superhero Collective for endless laughs and mischief. Thank you to the organizations and spaces who've carved out space for me to write: Northeast Ohio Master of Fine Arts, Twelve Literary Arts, and Juniper Summer Writing Institute.

Many thanks to the editors of the following publications, where a number of these poems first appeared, sometimes in different forms.

"American Beings," *Adroit Journal*

"Summertime," *Cosmonauts Avenue*

"Self-Interrogation," *Cotton Xenomorph*

"In a Dream, I Get Married in an Abandoned Mall," *Crazyhorse*

"Palestine," *Defunkt Magazine*

"I Buried My Brother Last Winter" and "I Call My Mother from the Moon," *Hampden-Sydney Poetry Review*

"In Which the White Woman on My Thesis Defense Asks Me About *Witness*," *Hobart*

"Ode," *Jellyfish Magazine*

"I Should Have Broken Up with My Ex," *[PANK]*

"Fuck Your Lecture on Craft, My People Are Dying," "Breaking [News]," *Poetry*

"Thirst," "All My Plants Are Dead," "I Once Looked in a Mirror but Couldn't See My Body," *The Rumpus*

"Poem in Which My Mother Tells Me Not to Do A Pap Smear Because It Might Tear My Nonexistent Hymen," *Underblong Poetry Journal*

"The Shell of a Cactus Fruit," *Winter Tangerine*

NOTES

"Good Muslims Are All Around Us," "Virginity for Sale," and "Dangerous Business" borrow lines from headlines from various national and international newspapers.

ABOUT THE AUTHOR

Noor Hindi (she/her/hers) is a Palestinian American poet and reporter. She is a 2021 Ruth Lilly and Dorothy Sargent Rosenberg Poetry Fellow. *DEAR GOD. DEAR BONES. DEAR YELLOW.* is her debut collection of poems. She lives in Dearborn. Follow her on Twitter @MyNrhindi.

ABOUT HAYMARKET BOOKS

Haymarket Books is a radical, independent, nonprofit book publisher based in Chicago.

Our mission is to publish books that contribute to struggles for social and economic justice. We strive to make our books a vibrant and organic part of social movements and the education and development of a critical, engaged, international left.

We take inspiration and courage from our namesakes, the Haymarket martyrs, who gave their lives fighting for a better world. Their 1886 struggle for the eight-hour day—which gave us May Day, the international workers' holiday—reminds workers around the world that ordinary people can organize and struggle for their own liberation. These struggles continue today across the globe—struggles against oppression, exploitation, poverty, and war.

Since our founding in 2001, Haymarket Books has published more than five hundred titles. Radically independent, we seek to drive a wedge into the risk-averse world of corporate book publishing. Our authors include Noam Chomsky, Arundhati Roy, Rebecca Solnit, Angela Y. Davis, Howard Zinn, Amy Goodman, Wallace Shawn, Mike Davis, Winona LaDuke, Ilan Pappé, Richard Wolff, Dave Zirin, Keeanga-Yamahtta Taylor, Nick Turse, Dahr Jamail, David Barsamian, Elizabeth Laird, Amira Hass, Mark Steel, Avi Lewis, Naomi Klein, and Neil Davidson. We are also the trade publishers of the acclaimed Historical Materialism Book Series, of Dispatch Books, and of the Voice of Witness Book Series.

www.ingramcontent.com/pod-product-compliance
Lightning Source LLC
LaVergne TN
LVHW020542171224
799297LV00002B/248